ESSAYS IN INTERNATIONAL FINANCE

No. 155, October 1984

—————

MANAGING THE WORLD ECONOMY: WILL WE EVER LEARN?

—————

STEPHEN MARRIS

D1029599

INTERNATIONAL FINANCE SECTION

DEPARTMENT OF ECONOMICS

PRINCETON UNIVERSITY

Princeton, New Jersey

ESSAYS IN INTERNATIONAL FINANCE

ESSAYS IN INTERNATIONAL FINANCE are published by the International Finance Section of the Department of Economics of Princeton University. The Section sponsors this series of publications, but the opinions expressed are those of the authors. The Section welcomes the submission of manuscripts for publication in this and its other series, PRINCETON STUDIES IN INTERNATIONAL FINANCE and SPECIAL PAPERS IN INTERNATIONAL ECONOMICS. See the Notice to Contributors at the back of this Essay.

The author of this Essay, Stephen Marris, is a Senior Fellow at the Institute for International Economics in Washington. Before that, he spent twenty-seven years in Paris with the Organization for Economic Cooperation and Development, for the last eight years as Economic Adviser to the Secretary-General. He was the first editor of the *OECD Economic Outlook* and has been closely involved with the work of the OECD's Economic Policy Committee and its Working Party No. 3. This Essay, his second contribution to this series, was presented as the Frank D. Graham Memorial Lecture at Princeton University on May 3, 1984.

PETER B. KENEN, *Director*
International Finance Section

ESSAYS IN INTERNATIONAL FINANCE

No. 155, October 1984

MANAGING THE WORLD ECONOMY: WILL WE EVER LEARN?

STEPHEN MARRIS

INTERNATIONAL FINANCE SECTION

DEPARTMENT OF ECONOMICS

PRINCETON UNIVERSITY

Princeton, New Jersey

INTERNATIONAL FINANCE SECTION
EDITORIAL STAFF

Library of Congress Cataloging in Publication Data

Marris, Stephen.
  Managing the world economy.

  (The Frank D. Graham memorial lecture; 1984 May 3) (Essays in international finance, ISSN 0071-142X; no. 155)
  "May 3, 1984."
  Bibliography: p.
  1. Economic policy—Addresses, essays, lectures.   2. Fiscal policy—Addresses, essays, lectures.   3. International economic integration—Addresses, essays, lectures.   4. Economics—Addresses, essays, lectures.
  I. Title.   II. Series.   III. Series: Essays in international finance; no. 155.
HG136.P7   no. 155   332′.042s   84-19344   [HD82]
ISBN 0-88165-062-5   [338.9]

Printed in the United States of America by Princeton University Press at Princeton, New Jersey.

International Standard Serial Number: 0071-142X

International Standard Book Number: 0-88165-062-5

Library of Congress Catalog Card Number: 84-19344

CONTENTS

Managing the World Economy: Will We Ever Learn?

To be invited to give the Frank D. Graham Memorial Lecture is not only a great honor; it has provided me with a welcome opportunity to try to make some sense out of my close involvement in the management of free-market economies over the past thirty years.

Looking back, two things strike me forcibly. The first is the fickleness of conventional economic wisdom. The second is the very close relationship between economic orthodoxy as it relates to domestic economic policy and economic orthodoxy as it relates to the need for—and particularly the nature of—international economic cooperation. Having traced these out, I shall try to set out some of the lessons I believe we should draw from this experience. I shall conclude with some somewhat unflattering remarks about the economics profession.

The Fickleness of Conventional Economic Wisdom

The fickleness of conventional economic wisdom can be caricatured by a set of antitheses. When I began my career at the Organization for Economic Cooperation and Development in 1956,[1] conventional wisdom had it that the government's primary responsibility was to provide the right level of aggregate monetary demand; if it did so, the supply side would look after itself. Before I left the OECD, it was increasingly being argued that if we got the supply side right, demand would look after itself.

I refer not so much to the extreme form of supply-side economics associated with the name of Arthur Laffer but to the much more intellectually respectable arguments, based on neoclassical economics, that underlie much recent German economic thought and policymaking and are exerting a spreading influence. To get the supply side right, according to this school, it is necessary to raise the rate of return on investment by slowing down the growth of real wages and to lower the real rate of interest by reducing budget deficits. These moves, it is said, will in time lead to more demand, whereas, according to earlier conventional wisdom, they would lead to less.

A second antithesis. During the first half of my career, it was increasingly accepted that fiscal policy was by far the government's most powerful tool

[1] Then the Organization for European Economic Cooperation.

1

for influencing the course of aggregate demand. For example, in a 1966 report Working Party 3 of the OECD stated:

> In the field of demand management, it is agreed that it should be a general objective of fiscal and monetary policies . . . to promote a continuing expansion of total national expenditure in line with the trend growth of productive potential. There is also agreement that, in general, fiscal policy should play a major role in the mangement of demand. (par. 42)

Monetary policy was assigned a subordinate role. The monetary authorities were expected to maintain an appropriate level of nominal interest rates, given the fiscal-policy stance, and it was assumed—sometimes explicitly, often only implicitly—that such rates could be achieved without injecting excessive liquidity into the system. The influential Radcliffe Report (1959) observed:

> Fiscal measures have the advantage over monetary measures in having a more certain impact. (par. 516) . . . We envisage the use of monetary measures as not in ordinary times playing other than a subordinate part in guiding the . . . economy. (par. 511) . . . Control over the 'money supply'—whatever that may be made to mean—is not by itself a reliable policy measure. (par. 504) . . . The more flexible the fiscal measures can be made the less it will be necessary to rely on monetary measures. (par. 517)

But, in a premonition of things to come, it went on:

> On the other hand, if the authorities are unable to manipulate taxation with sufficient flexibility, there will have to be more reliance on monetary measures. (par. 517)

Again, by the time I left the OECD these propositions had been more or less turned upside down. In several of the major industrial countries, policy has come to be based on the view that control over the rate of growth of the money supply is virtually the sole instrument that a government should use to discharge its responsibility for the level of prices and aggregate demand. Current conventional wisdom about fiscal policy is somewhat less clear-cut, although there is a distinct tendency in some countries to subordinate it to monetary-policy objectives. In the United Kingdom, for example, the path set out for fiscal policy in the Medium Term Financial Strategy has been determined explicitly in terms of the need to achieve a given outcome for the growth of the money supply. The same role reversal is evident in Germany, where the main thrust of fiscal policy is to reduce the structural budget deficit in order to reduce real interest rates.

The academic profession has gone even further. Enthusiastic followers of the rational-expectations hypothesis have demonstrated, very elegantly, that if everyone understood the ultimate consequences of fiscal action as well as

2

they did, then, logically, such actions could have no effect at all on the level of aggregate demand. It is true that this view has not been widely embraced by the profession and, despite much empirical work, it does not appear to fit the facts (see Feldstein, 1982).[2] But, with this amount of confusion being generated by the academic profession, it is perhaps hardly surprising that certain very highly placed policymakers in the United States should currently be arguing that there is no relationship between budget deficits and interest rates—at the same time that they claim credit for the expansionary stimulus generated by those deficits.

These changes in conventional wisdom about the conduct of macroeconomic policy have been accompanied by almost equally dramatic changes in views about the nature and even the direction of many key behavioral relationships. In earlier days, it was widely held that the Phillips curve was a reasonably stable relationship that provided the touchstone for steering the economy between the pitfalls of inflation and deflation. Today, it is not only accepted that this relationship is distinctly unstable, but it is also argued by some that over any period relevant to policy making the curve is actually vertical. In other words, for all practical purposes it does not exist.

Take another example. Twenty years ago, we believed that investment was largely driven by the accelerator. Evidence was marshaled to show that the influence of actual and expected demand very largely dominated any influence coming from interest rates or rates of return. The same Radcliffe Report (1959, par. 464) commented, "It does not seem that changes in interest rates . . . have had much ultimate effect on the demand for goods." Today, as noted, policies in some countries are implicitly or explicitly based on the assumption that the reverse is true.

This reversal relates to another area where there has been a significant change in conventional wisdom. Throughout the whole period, academic theory concerning the distribution of income between labor and capital has been in a somewhat confused state and has generally not performed well when it came to empirical verification. The field was thus left open to pragmatists. So during the 1950s and 1960s it came to be accepted wisdom that businessmen were always in a position to set prices at a margin over costs that would provide them with a rate of return at which they would be happy to invest more. The Organization for European Economic Cooperation, in a 1961 report, stated: "The share of labor, apart from cyclical shifts, has remained remarkably constant in almost all countries since around 1950.

---

[2] As so often happens with economic thought, the rational-expectations hypothesis is not a new idea. Feldstein (p. 2) attributes the revival of what he calls the "pre-Ricardian equivalence hypothesis" to, among others, M. J. Bailey, R. Barro, and J. R. Tanner.

3

With high employment, business has been able to maintain profit margins . . ." (OEEC, 1961, p. 53; see also Dow, 1964, Chap. XIII).

This meant that, with generally low or negative real interest rates, investment would respond very strongly to increased demand, as, indeed, it did. In one way, this was a good thing. For, once we had got through the immediate postwar reconstruction period, we found ourselves for about twenty years in a world in which output was not constrained by capacity limitations, only by the supply of labor. But the other side of the coin was that demand-induced bursts of investment were one of the principal reasons why inflation originating in the labor market was steadily ratcheted up from one cyclical peak to the next.

Even before 1973, there was isolated evidence of a downward secular shift in the share of profits. But it was only after the first oil crisis that this shift became a fairly general phenomenon. And, slowly and unevenly, attention began shifting toward more classical economic theory, with its emphasis on the relationship between real rates of return and real interest rates, and on the role of relative factor prices in determining both the level of output and the amount of employment associated with a given level of output. By 1977, Malinvaud (1977; see also 1982) had provided a formal framework for the coexistence of Keynesian and classical unemployment, and there is now a substantial literature on this subject running from Giersch (1979) and Sachs (1979) to Artus (1984). Empirical evidence appears to support the "disequilibrium-real-wage hypothesis," although it is slightly disconcerting to note that the countries identified as suffering from this problem differ among the studies. There has also been a revival of interest in the role of real wages in the 1930s (see, e.g., Sachs, 1983, pp. 271-274). And such is the lagged but intimate connivance among events, ideas, and action that, by 1984, a British Chancellor of the Exchequer had introduced a budget which, by increasing taxes on capital (investment) and reducing them on labor, turned another piece of conventional postwar wisdom on its head.

Managing the World Economy

More examples could be given of the almost complete reversal over the past thirty years of the conventional wisdom about domestic macroeconomic policy. But let us turn now to international economic policy. Inevitably, the evolution of ideas has centered around the exchange-rate regime, as the most direct interface between sovereign economic policies. It is fascinating to reread the heated debate between advocates of fixed or flexible rates that runs through the first Princeton Essays in International Finance.

What emerges is that there is a lot of common ground on the issues of economic analysis involved. Graham (1943) could accept as an ideal solution fixed rates between countries that maintained monetary stability; he just did not think that this was very likely. On the other side, Nurske (1945) could accept that "the external balance of payments should not require an individual country to . . . undergo either . . . inflation . . . or . . . deflation. . . . It is the exchange rate that should be changed . . ." (p. 24). But he also argued: "Barring inflationary developments in individual countries such adjustments should not be necessary except at infrequent intervals (say, five, ten, or fifteen years)" (p. 22).

In retrospect, the decision to go for fixed rates was probably based less on economic doctrine than on a broader philosophical approach to international economic management. After the disasters of the 1930s, it seemed unwise to assume that national governments could be trusted to act consistently in the collective interest. An internationalist—but also elitist—approach was needed. We (the elite) would meet in international organizations created for the purpose to decide how the international economy should be managed. Thus, although it was widely accepted that exchange rates could not remain fixed forever, it seemed natural to give an important role to an international bureaucracy in decisions about when and by how much they should be changed.

Behind this approach there was often the hidden hope that some form of supranational political authority would gradually evolve to legitimize this transfer of economic sovereignty. As this did not happen, it is all the more surprising that fixed rates became such a widely and deeply entrenched dogma in official circles. To its credit, the academic profession never lost sight of the fact that, in Graham's (1949, p. 3) words, "Exchange rates are prices," and eventually it launched a successful counterattack.

Once the decision had been taken to go for fixed exchange rates, both the need for, and the nature of, international economic management followed logically from the conventional wisdom of the day about domestic economic management. The major countries had a collective responsibility to maintain the right level of demand in the world economy as a whole. If the sense of the meeting was that the risks were on the inflationary side, then some countries should take restrictive action, essentially of a fiscal nature. And conversely if the risks were on the deflationary side.

Moreover, since it was assumed that "we" were keeping exchange rates more or less where they should be, then, if the risks were on the inflationary side, it was the countries with balance-of-payments deficits that should take restrictive action. And if the risks were on the deflationary side, it was the countries in balance-of-payments surplus that should take expansionary

5

action. This was the logical thread running through the Bretton Woods agreements, echoes of which could still be heard in the 1970s, as in the so-called "McCracken Report" (OECD, 1977, p. 30):

Policymakers should communicate and consult with one another as a matter of intelligent self-interest. They should regularly try to form a view as to the need to stimulate or restrain demand in the world economy as a whole. Countries which should take the lead in expanding demand are those with high unemployment, low inflation, favorable balances of payments, large reserves and good creditworthiness. The converse obtains if overall restraint is what is required.

(The McCracken Report, written by a group of economists with widely different backgrounds, is of considerable historical interest. It is clear, in retrospect, that they were trying to build bridges between the Keynesian consensus, which was by then well into its decline, and the monetarist/ neoclassical consensus, which was very much on the rise. Sadly, but perhaps inevitably, the report was unpopular in both camps.)

For quite a time, in the 1950s and 1960s, this approach seemed to be working rather well, even though there was considerable slippage between theory and practice. But we did not, of course, succeed in keeping real exchange rates where they should have been. "Dilemma cases" emerged, most notably the United States in the 1960s, "where demand pressures are not inappropriate, but where the current balance is nevertheless out of line . . . because of imperfectly adjusted competitive positions"—a nice euphemism! (OECD, 1966, par. 46). We nevertheless soldiered on, and in so doing provided Mundell (1962) with the opportunity to develop an analytical framework in which monetary policy could be assigned to external objectives and fiscal policy to internal objectives. As Working Party 3 of the OECD (1966, par. 47) put it:

A country in surplus because of large capital receipts should normally adopt an easier monetary policy than might otherwise have been appropriate. . . . Assuming that the general demand-supply situation is roughly in balance, the adoption of an easier monetary policy would usually call for some tightening of fiscal policy. . . . A country in deficit because of substantial capital outflows should normally adopt a tighter monetary policy than might otherwise be appropriate . . . and this may involve complementary changes in fiscal policy.

It is also worth noting that with an increasing number of observations we were gradually able to develop empirical tools that tracked quite well how the fixed-rate system was working. This was true not only for the price and income elasticities affecting trade and current balances, but also for capital flows, where we were able to draw on the work by Branson (1971) and others on portfolio-balance theory. Indeed, I still remember with some pride papers we produced in the late 1960s that gave forecasts running all the way from GNP, through prices and interest rates, to trade balances and capital flows, ending up with changes in official-settlements balances and likely claims on the U.S. gold stock.[3]

It would be hard to exaggerate how completely this conventional wisdom about international macroeconomic management had been overturned by the early 1980s—although this is still often obscured by ritual references to the virtues of economic cooperation.

The intellectual origins of this sea change are fairly easy to trace. Working from floating exchange rates, it is possible to develop essentially static general-equilibrium models in which, with instantaneous adjustment in all markets, the impact on other countries of changes in prices or demand in one country is fully neutralized. In such models, economic relations between nations are left to be determined—as they should be—solely by real structural parameters, such as propensities to save and invest, the real rate of return on capital, and the supply curve of labor. Friedman (1953) and Johnson (1969) made major contributions to the revival of this approach to international economics, arguing that, under floating exchange rates, countries would and should recover their monetary autonomy. And once again, with a lag, the implications began to show up as conventional wisdom in official and governmental thinking. The slogan thus became: "If each country gets its fundamentals right, the world will look after itself." Indeed, this philosophy was partly incorporated into the Second Amendment to the Articles of the International Monetary Fund.

This change in the conceptual approach to international cooperation was part of a wider change in attitude toward the management of free-market economies, which is well captured in the aphorism: "Governments do not solve problems, they are the problem." At the international level, moreover, the case for the kind of elitist approach described earlier was to some extent undermined by its own apparently brilliant success. As a quarter of a century rolled by with almost uninterrupted growth, expanding trade, and no major breakdowns, memories of the horrors of the 1930s faded. Problems of national economic management gradually reoccupied center stage, especially in the 1970s, when the perplexities of stagflation became a central element in the intellectual and political debate.

It is no doubt natural that in this changed climate there should be a resurgence of the philosophical approach to international economic rela-

---

[3] Fairly detailed forecasts of capital flows and official financing were contained in confidential documents produced for Working Party 3 of the OECD, particularly in the period 1969-71. These forecasts were described and discussed in qualitative terms in contemporary issues of the *OECD Economic Outlook* (see, in particular, No. 5, pp. 33-59; No. 6, pp. 32-54; No. 9, pp. 25-39; and No. 11, pp. 29-40).

tions so evident in Graham's writings. Believing passionately in the virtues of maximum freedom for individuals within the national economy, this school has always tended to argue that the same should apply to sovereign states in the world economy. And, indeed, models can be produced in which world welfare is maximized when each country independently pursues its perceived interests, so long as it is fully informed about the intentions of others and how they will react to any course of action it takes. This school thus tends to argue that this informational role furnishes the only justification for the existence of international organizations.

As a matter of fact, even this qualification was challenged by Harry Johnson and others who, while extolling the virtues of private markets, argued, probably rightly, that meetings of national officials and governments can be subject to bandwagon effects, leading to collective misinformation and overenthusiastic crusades against the currently perceived enemy, be it unemployment, inflation, OPEC, or poverty. Some, like Vaubel (1983, p. 18) see international organizations in an even darker light:

> It is well known . . . that, to some extent, rational politicians and bureaucrats have an incentive and the power . . . to act against . . . the welfare of society at large. What is only gradually coming to be known is that international collusion strengthens this power.

Thus, in a remarkably short space of time the international economic organizations have gone from being regarded as one of the brightest of man's creations, paving the way toward an evolutionary absorption of national economic sovereignty into a wider collectivity of interests, to being regarded, at best, as clearinghouses for the exchange of information or, at worst, as having a negative influence on world economic welfare.[4]

This statement may seem much exaggerated at a time when the International Monetary Fund is playing such an important and valuable role in dealing with the debt crisis. But that role is essentially an exercise in crisis management and bears little resemblance to what was understood by economic cooperation in earlier years. What is striking is that, while the Fund's influence on the policies of third-world debtor countries has greatly increased, its influence—and that of the wider network of international institutions—on the policies of the major industrial countries has virtually vanished. Today, it is commonly said that there never was such an influence—another example of rewriting history. Both France and the United Kingdom had to

---

[4] This Essay is focused on the management of the world economy at the macroeconomic level. At the microeconomic level, conventional economic wisdom has stood up much better to the test of time. There has not been the same *conceptual* erosion of the role assigned to international organizations to promote and police the maximum freedom for international trade and payments. Indeed, this assignment has held up surprisingly well to the intense political pressures generated by poor macroeconomic performance since 1973.

make conditional drawings from the Fund and, for at least twenty-five years after World War II, German and Japanese policies were strongly influenced by their desire to be "accepted" by the international community. The influence on American policies was, on the whole, less, but by no means negligible (see Solomon, 1977).

The change in attitude toward the international organizations has perhaps been most marked in the United States. But it is increasingly shared by the other members of the Group of Five, or "Versailles Group," with the exception of France, even if the language they use to express it pays more lip service to earlier conventional wisdom.

It is, of course, hard for those of us who have worked most of our lives in international organizations to realize that it was all a mistake. And we have been slow to respond to—or even fully grasp—the case now made against us. To give a constructive answer it is essential to distinguish the philosophical from the conceptual and factual basis of the new consensus. Reasonable people are always likely to differ about the proper role and function of government, and the consensus will no doubt continue to evolve in hard-to-predict ways over the decades to come. But the case for greatly restricting the role previously assigned to the international organizations with respect to macroeconomic policy also rests on the empirical validity of the general-equilibrium models in which floating exchange rates neutralize external shocks. I will return to this question later.

How Did It Happen?

I hope enough has been said to justify my two initial propositions: that conventional economic wisdom has proved very fickle over the last thirty years, and that there has been a striking parallelism between accepted doctrines regarding the management of market economies at the national and international levels.

The picture is obviously overdrawn, however. The prevailing consensus was never unanimous, and the dramatic changes did not occur in a vacuum. At each point in the story, there was a respectable body of minority opinion—monetarists during the Keynesian era, Keynesians during the monetarist era. Furthermore, conventional wisdom was colored in each country by its own history and intellectual traditions. Even at the height of the Keynesian consensus, German economic thought and policymaking continued to give more emphasis to monetary discipline. Even at the height of the flexible-rate consensus, French thinking remained strongly attached to the idea that the State, rather than private citizens, should determine a country's exchange rate.

More important has been the fascinating interplay among ideas, policies,

9

and events. Looking back, it is easy to see how ideas, with a lag, influenced policies; how policies, with a lag, influenced events; and how events, with a lag, changed ideas. It would take too long to trace this out in detail. It is most obvious in the shift in concern from unemployment to inflation. In 1942, Graham wrote, "Men are genuinely afraid that peace may . . . break out" (1942, p. 246). Four years later, he wrote, "if we . . . are so inept as to permit wide-scale unemployment, we shall suffer, and will deserve, the totalitarian fate we fought to avoid" (1946, p. 59). He was convinced, with many others, that "it is . . . within the government's power to set the level of total expenditures . . . wherever it will. It follows . . . that the government can set it at that optimum level which will provide full employment with a stable price level" (1946, pp. 40-41). Nobody can say what he would have written forty years later, but, given the concern about price stability that runs through his work, it seems probable that the emphasis would have been very different.

Take another example. During my time at the OECD, the ratio of public expenditure to GNP in the OECD area rose from 25 to 42 per cent. And with rising welfare benefits and falling tax thresholds, marginal tax/benefit ratios [5] rose to phenomenal levels. It is hardly surprising, therefore, that attention shifted sharply from the supposed positive externalities of the welfare state to its supposed negative impact on incentives to work, save, and invest.

Again, at the international level, it is clear that we badly mismanaged the adjustable-peg exchange-rate system built into the Bretton Woods agreements. It is equally clear that this is one of several factors that contributed to the ratcheting up of inflation that brought the golden era of the 1950s and 1960s to an end. And it was these events that swung the consensus toward flexible rates.

Many more examples could be given of the way in which the course of events appears to justify the change in conventional wisdom. But the question still remains as to whether, as members of the economics profession, we can really justify such radical 180-degree changes as have occurred.

The Verdict of History

The noneconomist historian, reviewing this period, might well be tempted to draw rather unflattering conclusions about our profession. Using our own terminology, he might unkindly suggest that the elasticity of conventional economic wisdom with respect to events appears, after a lag, to have been

[5] I.e., the ratio of increases in pre- to post-tax incomes after allowing for the loss of means-tested and other discretionary social benefits.

very close to one. He might raise doubts as to whether, on the record, economics has yet become a mature science that can assimilate new observations constructively into an agreed body of thought. Or, trying to be fair, he might suggest that if there is such a body of progressively evolving established doctrine, then economists appear to have been singularly unsuccessful in getting it across to public opinion and political leaders. Being nasty, he could point to the proliferation of jokes along the lines of "Ask five economists and you'll get six opinions."

Turning to his own subject, our historian might go on to suggest that economists exhibit one of the classic symptoms of those unsure of their legitimacy: they start to rewrite history. Almost any economic history written before 1973, when trying to explain the historically unique successes of the postwar period, attributed an important role to national and international demand management. In the view of the authors of a 1968 OECD report, for example:

> In the post-war period, discussion in organizations such as the OECD, the International Monetary Fund and the European Economic Community have . . . played an important part in helping countries to evolve more adequate demand management policies. . . . As experience has been gained . . . a sort of continuous watch on the international adjustment process is being developed. . . . We have no doubt that international cooperation of this sort should and will be strengthened as time goes on and that national stabilization policies will, to their benefit, be increasingly conducted within this framework. (par. 265)

Now this is increasingly rejected, it being argued that the postwar liberal economic order created a spontaneous and self-sustaining investment boom generated by the need to make up for wartime devastation and catch up with American technology (e.g., Wolf, 1983)—as if we had not had wars to recover from, or somebody's technology to catch up with, before!

A Determinist View

The historian might well go further. He might suggest that if only economists had a proper training in history and could lift their eyes from their computers, they would see that we may be reaching a point of inflection in a cycle of interaction between events and ideas concerning the key issues of macroeconomic policy that goes back at least as far as World War I; and that, if so, we could well be heading for another complete reversal, with a new consensus emerging in favor of fixed exchange rates and activist demand-management policies.

It may seem strange to suggest this when policies based on the existing consensus have brought us into the second year of a world recovery com-

11

bining, in the aggregate, a moderately respectable growth rate and stable or declining inflation. But then this is a strange recovery. The necessary crusade against inflation has got caught up in a rather confusing way in the current consensus favoring national autonomy for policymaking. Under the slogan of "convergence," the key countries have, indeed, achieved convergence of inflation rates at low levels. But, paradoxically, convergence of inflation rates is not a necessary condition in the floating-exchange-rate models that have been so influential in the emergence of this consensus.

To add to the confusion, under this same slogan of convergence, we have seen the most *divergent* set of fiscal policies since World War II. While it is widely known that the United States has taken discretionary fiscal action in an expansionary direction amounting to several percentage points of GNP, it is much less widely realized that, quantitatively, Japan, Germany, and the United Kingdom have taken even greater discretionary action in the opposite direction.[6] The confusion seems at times to have been apparent to those involved in it. Talking to journalists on December 6, 1982, Secretary of the Treasury Donald Regan remarked:

> If we're going to have this where one nation is doing one thing and another nation is doing something else and a third nation is doing its thing, rather than trying to all be in the same general mode, traders who are trying to trade these currencies are not going to know what's going on. . . . There is a need to look at the problems that exist in the international financial world in a concerted fashion. . . . We have not discussed this nor have we held meetings on it. . . .

Divergent fiscal policies are, of course, consistent with the philosophy that each country should "do its own thing." Indeed, it is important to realize that Prime Ministers Thatcher and Nakasone and Chancellor Kohl have committed their political fortunes just as firmly to the proposition that the chief aim of macroeconomic policy must be to reduce budget deficits as President Reagan appears to have committed his to the view that the overriding priority must be to increase defense expenditures and reduce taxes. The result has inevitably been the most unbalanced recovery since World War II, and the prospect that within a year or two the United States will become a net debtor nation. Our historian might conclude that, however creditworthy the United States may now seem, it will eventually lose the confidence of its creditors. Confidence can then be restored only by monetary and fiscal overkill of the kind that became necessary—and has

[6] According to estimates made by the OECD (1983, Table 10), the cyclically adjusted budget deficit of the United States will have increased by 1½ percentage points of GNP over the four years 1980-84, while that of Japan will have been *reduced* by 3 percentage points and that of the four largest European countries by over 2 percentage points.

been widely applauded—in, for example, Britain in 1976 and 1981, Belgium in 1982, or Mexico in 1983.

He could go on to suggest that the other major countries, which have been complacently enjoying the demand stimulus coming from U.S. budget and current-account deficits, will be slow to respond when this source of expansion is rather abruptly reversed. After all, current conventional wisdom holds that attempts to coordinate macroeconomic policies internationally—as at the Bonn Summit—would be misguided. A not implausible scenario could emerge in which there is a strong surge of interest rates in the United States, a sharp drop in the dollar, and a new recession in the North, accentuated by a new debt crisis in the South.

From there, our historian needs only a lively imagination to conjure up the picture of a Summit Meeting from which the heads of state emerge to announce that they have agreed that there is something wrong somewhere. To restore stability to the international monetary system, they have decided to fix exchange rates at "sensible" levels; to halt the renewed rise in unemployment, they have agreed to reduce interest rates and embark on internationally coordinated fiscal reflation.

This may well be a fantasy. But the risk of an *overreaction* against today's conventional wisdom is sufficiently high to present a real challenge to our profession. The various strands of economic thought that have strongly influenced policymaking at different times over the past thirty years almost all have respectable intellectual antecedents going back over a hundred years. And, in relation to particular circumstances and time horizons, they nearly all contain important elements of truth. We have now had many years of extraordinarily varied experience in the application of these ideas to the real world. On a cross-country comparative basis we have almost a surfeit of empirical data to work with. What is needed is not so much new theories as a better synthesis of what we should already know, so as to provide a more consistent basis for policymaking over the years, less susceptible to the changing tides of fashion. So let me conclude by trying to set out some of the lessons that I would like to think can be drawn from this experience.

The Unanswerable Questions

It would be helpful if we could first agree that there are two key questions to which we will probably never have definitive answers.

First, we have no definitive answer to inflation. We simply do not know the extent to which it is possible to exploit the extraordinary productive potential of a system of decentralized wage and price decisions under con-

13

ditions of rapidly increasing demand without so far undermining confidence in the value of money as to force us to retreat. By now, moreover, we should have learned to look with great suspicion at ideas that purport to provide a painless way to reconcile relative price flexibility with overall price stability.

Considerable efforts have been made to deal with this problem through price and incomes policy. In certain circumstances and in certain countries, this approach may have some validity. But those of us who at one time hoped that it could be used to modify individual behavior to better serve the collective interest are sadder and wiser today. The same should be true of those who, under the influence of the rational-expectations hypothesis, became convinced that a firm commitment to the progressive reduction of publicly announced targets for the growth of the money supply could painlessly reduce inflation without depressing output. It is true that under flexible exchange rates, monetary restraint, through its effect on the real exchange rate, has become a much more powerful short-run anti-inflationary tool for any individual country. But we have learned that this is no solution for the world as a whole. And even for the country concerned, the benefits have usually proved ephemeral.

Where does this leave us? For over twenty years we were able to combine a historically unprecedented growth rate with only a relatively slowly accelerating rate of inflation. Even at the time, however, we knew that as each year of comparative success went by, the tradeoff was tilting against us. More recently, for over a decade, we have clearly, and more or less deliberately, failed to exploit fully this latent productive potential. The results are now evident. Price-wage equations fitted in the 1960s increasingly showed positive residuals toward the end of the period. Similar equations fitted to the late 1970s and early 1980s increasingly yield negative residuals (OECD, 1983, p. 50).

But how quickly could these recent anti-inflationary gains be reversed? Once again, we simply do not know. The record shows that the Phillips curve is not vertical over any time horizon relevant to policymaking. There *is* a tradeoff between growth and inflation over both the short and medium run, but it is inherently unstable. It is just as much nonsense to say that we must first defeat inflation and then we can grow as it is to say, let us grow now and worry about inflation later. We have no option but to go on learning through trial and error. In doing so, however, we should keep firmly in mind what we have learned: the rewards, in terms of productivity and welfare gains, that a free-market economy can generate under conditions of fast growth are enormous, but so are the costs of growing too fast. Hence the need for caution.

There is a second unanswerable question. We simply do not know the extent to which sociological and political forces at work in democratic societies can irreversibly impair the efficiency of market economies. Our massive development of social legislation and regulation over the last thirty years has certainly put this question to the test. Yet, despite much hard work, it has proved remarkably difficult to identify and measure large adverse effects on economic incentives. But there is a strong *a priori* case for believing that such effects could be significant, there is a good deal of circumstantial evidence, and the empirical work may be muddied by long lags. It is therefore understandable that reasonable people differ as to how far the poor economic performance of the last decade can be attributed to developments at the microeconomic—as opposed to the macroeconomic—level.

At the same time, the democratic process has responded, with a lag, bringing to power governments dedicated to deregulation, to restraining and reforming the welfare state, and—using European terminology—to reducing "rigidities." But I would contend that we have no way of knowing with any certainty just how much damage has been done or how far it may prove irreversible. Olson (1982) has pointed out forcefully that the role of private interest groups is just as important as the role of governments. And, as Attali (1981, Part 2) has shown, signs of a secular shift away from profits in the 1970s have given new life to economists in the West with a Marxist background, like Aglietta (1977) and Lipietz (1982), who stress the irreversible nature of the sociopolitical evolution of the capitalist system.

The record shows that governments have significant powers to redistribute personal incomes, albeit through a "leaky bucket." But it also suggests that, once we give up hope on incomes policy, they have little direct leverage on the distribution of income between capital and labor. They can tinker with the tax system, as the United States and the United Kingdom have recently done (in opposite directions). But the record suggests that what happens in the end, after tax shifting, will be strongly influenced by the balance of socioeconomic bargaining power. Recent events, it is true, show that the distribution of income can be indirectly shifted back toward profits, as postulated by neoclassical economics, by holding down aggregate demand and creating an excess supply of labor. But the lags appear to be agonizingly long, and the initial impact may well be perverse.

Where does this leave us? In many countries, further efforts are needed to slow down or reverse the rise in public expenditure. Much remains to be done to correct the excesses of state intervention at the microeconomic level. Distortions in our tax systems need to be removed. And the oversimplified version of the Keynesian approach, which concentrated exclusively

15

on the relationship between monetary demand and output and prices, must be extended to take into account the importance of real rates of return on financial and real assets, and of relative factor prices.

But, ultimately, governments cannot legislate changes in human behavior or restore the pristine characteristics of capitalist man if that is not what he wants. What we have seen clearly is how strongly the behavior of both private interest groups and governments is influenced by macroeconomic conditions. Under conditions of low inflation, fast growth, low unemployment, and well-aligned exchange rates, the trend has generally been away from the most pernicious forms of government intervention and private restrictive practices. But once we have allowed serious macroeconomic disequilibria to emerge—be they misaligned exchange rates or excessive inflation, unemployment, real wages, or real interest rates—then the trend has gone the other way; and, at the same time, the potential adverse effects on incentive caused by otherwise desirable social legislation have clearly increased.

Answerable Questions

If these ideas are accepted, then surely it follows that governments should be encouraged to pay particular attention to the task for which they, and only they, are responsible—control over the aggregate level of monetary demand. Here, in particular, we should be able to draw some fairly clearcut lessons from postwar experience.

First, we have learned that, contrary to much of today's conventional wisdom, fiscal policy remains governments' most powerful and predictable tool to influence demand over the short to medium run. The evidence of the last two years is eloquent on this point. America has been following a strongly expansionary fiscal policy and is having a strong recovery. Most of the rest of the world has been following strongly restrictive fiscal policies, and, despite the significant spillover of demand from America, is having an unusually weak recovery.

Second, however, we are much more aware of the dangers involved in the use of this instrument. The shorter-term danger is that, as recovery gathers momentum after a fiscal stimulus, the government will find that the political processes impede it from reversing gears quickly enough to offset the rise in the private sector's propensity to invest and the fall in its propensity to save. The longer-term danger is that arguments justifying budget deficits and, a fortiori, increased budget deficits will be only too easily misused by the ever-present political forces lobbying for higher expendi-

16

ture and lower taxes. Moreover, the more the financial markets lose confidence in the govenment's political ability to reverse a discretionary fiscal stimulus or, more generally, to keep the country's public finances under control, the more the role of expectations emerges with a vengeance, and the more difficult it becomes to use fiscal policy for demand-management purposes.

These dangers arise from the nature of the political process, not from anything inherent in economic analysis. There is something distasteful, if not dishonest, about economists who, perhaps because they share these essentially political concerns, devote themselves to proving—and teaching their students—that fiscal policy does not work, when it so obviously does. Surely, what economists should be doing is to continue the valiant efforts of people like Herbert Stein, Walter Heller, Arthur Okun, Charles Schultze, Alice Rivlin, and Martin Feldstein to better educate political leaders and their electorates about how fiscal policy should be used: about the difference between actual and full-employment (or structural) budget deficits; about the crucial need to set the discretionary use of fiscal policy for demand-management purposes firmly into a medium-term framework that explicitly allows for both cyclical fluctuations and secular trends in private propensities to save and invest.

I turn now to monetary policy. We have learned—or rather relearned—that there is indeed a close interdependence between monetary and fiscal policy. We have learned that this interdependence needs to be carefully watched because of the powerful role of expectations in financial markets. In other words, the scope for "twisting" the mix of monetary and fiscal policies is much more limited than we once thought (see Chouraqui and Price, 1984). We have learned that it is a mistake to target nominal interest rates at times of rapid expansion and rising—but unmeasurable—inflationary expectations. More recently, we have learned, or should have learned, that it is a mistake to target monetary aggregates at times of deflation and rising—but unmeasurable—liquidity preference.

If all this means the end of the road for those who so distrust democratic institutions that they would rather be governed by mechanical rules, so be it. There is no reason why the rest of us should not believe that the monetary authorities, drawing on all the experience they have acquired, will become increasingly skillful at following policies that involve the exercise of some discretion. To do so, however, they must be able to be honest with the markets about what they are doing. They should not have to pander to currently fashionable theories culled from the academic profession. In particular, they should not have to appear to be completely agnostic about the desirable level of interest rates or the exchange rate. Nor should they have to demean themselves by redefining the money supply every time they want to make a discretionary change in policy.

Turning now to international economic management, what have we learned about exchange rates? It is fascinating to read what Graham (1943) wrote on this subject forty-one years ago at the end of an earlier quarter of a century's experience with both fixed and floating rates:

> Fixed exchange rates, along with uncoordinated movements in national price levels . . . , will always issue in cumulative dislocations in the structure of international trade and finance. [On the other hand,] movements in exchange relationships between perfectly free currencies . . . may . . lead to still greater, perhaps not so long sustained, but equally dangerous aberrations. [What is needed] is a functional flexibility in the exchange rate structure, that is to say, so much freedom of movement, and so much only, as is necessary . . . to promote equilibrium within an international system of independent national price structures. (p. 3)

Later he argued:

> The hitherto most promising procedure to this end is the establishment of a not too narrow zone of fluctuation about a moving norm based, at any moment, on the current relationship between national price levels or, what will usually be the same thing, on the requirements for long-term equilibrium. (p. 14)

[The "hitherto" in this sentence relates to the fact that Graham was a strong advocate of a commodity-gold reserve system. He believed such a system would greatly help to stabilize national price (and output) levels and lead either to fixed exchange rates or to "an automatic adjustment of all other rates to the current domestic purchasing power of the currencies concerned . . ." (1943, p. 21).]

Will we ever learn? Four decades later, one could hardly put it better, with all due deference to my colleague John Williamson (1983). We have, however, learned quite a lot more about how to go about it, and can do better than Graham's rather vague references to "an extension of the practices of the British Exchange Equalization Account . . . with such cooperation between the several national stabilization funds as could be voluntarily attained" (1943, p. 14).

First, we have learned that monetary policy has a very strong influence on today's capital flows and hence on flexible exchange rates. Second, we have learned that under flexible exchange rates the exchange rate becomes one of the most powerful channels of transmission from monetary policy to the level of domestic output and prices. Indeed, in the more open economies it appears to have become a more powerful and predictable channel than the traditional channels of liquidity, wealth, and interest rates. Recent

18

experience has shown, moreover, that this is increasingly true in the United States, albeit to a lesser extent than in more open economies.

At least on the Western side of the Atlantic, McKinnon (1984) has perhaps most insistently drawn the right conclusions from postwar monetary experience—although the importance of what he has been saying has often been obscured by his predilection for monetary rules and his neglect of fiscal policy. The lessons he has drawn are relatively straightforward. It is a mistake to implement monetary policy without regard for the domestic monetary consequences of international capital flows. Persistent movements of exchange rates away from longer-run equilibrium levels can often be a good indicator of the need for a discretionary change in monetary policy. Put the other way around, trying to keep the exchange rate within Graham's "zone of fluctuation" should be an explicit aim of monetary policy.[7] Finally, and most important, such discretionary monetary policies should be internationally coordinated among the central banks of the major countries, so as both to maximize the stabilizing impact on exchange rates and to ensure that, *taken together*, their policies are neither too inflationary nor too deflationary.

While the explicit adoption of these proposals, especially by the United States, would be an enormous step forward, it would not, by itself, be enough. This is vividly illustrated by the fact that McKinnon's rules would have required the United States to have followed an easier monetary policy in the recent past, at a time when the markets have been (rightly) obsessed with the danger that the Federal Reserve Board will in the end be forced to monetize excessively large structural budget deficits. It is clear, therefore, that fiscal policy must be brought into the picture, and that proper management of the world economy requires at least some degree of coordination of the fiscal policies of the major countries.

Here, again, oversimplified models have had an undue impact on conventional wisdom. If one assumes perfect substitutability between domestic and foreign financial assets, it follows that when one major country is running large structural budget deficits that are pushing it toward the "crowding-out frontier" at which private investment is choked off, all other countries will also find themselves pushed toward this frontier. According to this school, any crowding-out problem must be a worldwide phenomenon, almost by definition. This line of reasoning led to what was perhaps the

---

[7] These ideas are not new, of course. Indeed, after a brief period of benign neglect in the mid-1970s following the move to flexible rates, all the industrial countries *other than* the United States have, to varying degrees, been following exchange-rate-oriented monetary policies. The significance of McKinnon's internationalist views is that they come from an *American* economist, and one with strong monetarist leanings.

most dramatic reversal of conventional wisdom of all, the proposition that the right way to get out of a world recession was for all the major countries to reduce their structural budget deficits simultaneously. In a communiqué issued after the May 2, 1982, Ministerial Meeting, the Group of Ten reported:

> Ministers and Governors believed that a premature relaxation of the present anti-inflationary policy stance might jeopardize the results so far obtained. . . . They emphasized however, that a strengthening of fiscal discipline in both the near and medium term could foster economic recovery by relieving pressures on interest rates. (p. 149) [8]

One does not know whether to be thankful that the largest country of all resolutely refused to heed this advice. If the United States had followed it, we would at least have discovered rather quickly what was wrong with the theory. As it is, the present world constellation, combining unduly expansionary and unduly restrictive fiscal policies, in a sense cancels out. Two wrongs do not make a right, but they have given fortuitous support—and a temporary respite—to the thesis that each country should do its own thing as far as fiscal policy is concerned.

What we have, in fact, learned is that the international interactions between national fiscal policies are not easy to pin down. The degree of substitutability between domestic and foreign financial assets not only varies between currencies but is strongly conditioned by the past behavior of exchange rates and their expected future behavior. It is encouraging, therefore, that the considerable efforts made over recent years to build models of the present flexible-rate system in which exchange rates and interest rates are fully endogenized are beginning to pay off. It is particularly encouraging that these models show, as would be expected by those who have been following events closely since 1973, that there are important asymmetries among countries in the impact of monetary and fiscal actions, as well as crucially important differences in the impacts over the shorter and the longer run (Larsen, Llewellyn, and Potter, 1983; Yoshitomi, 1984).

This technical progress is also valuable in a much broader sense. These models demonstrate empirically something that should have been blindingly obvious all along. The static general-equilibrium models discussed earlier failed to take into account the very different lengths of the lags involved in the working out of longer-run income, price, and interest-rate elasticities in the real world. Nor did they take into account the fact that these lags are sufficiently long to allow the emergence of significant and

---

[8] Official thinking at this time was strongly influenced by a powerful speech on fiscal discipline that the Managing Director of the IMF had given to the American Enterprise Institute in March of that year (Larosière, 1982).

20

often perverse feedbacks from international to domestic price and output levels, and vice versa.

This means that short-term fluctuations in demand and prices *are* transmitted from country to country in the real world, even with flexible exchange rates. And this means that it would be pure luck if a set of independently determined national monetary and fiscal policies could optimize world welfare, even assuming perfect knowledge. It can be shown analytically that there will always be a constellation of policy settings, in which each country trades off changes in its monetary and fiscal policies against changes by others, under which every country will be better off in terms of its own perceived policy objectives (Hamada, 1974 and 1976; Johansen, 1982; Blanchard and Dornbusch, 1983; Cooper, forthcoming). Moreover, it can now be shown empirically that the values of the key parameters in the best existing models are such that "an uncoordinated selection of macroeconomic strategies is likely to lead to an inefficient mix of monetary and fiscal policies and to an inefficient overall stance on the level of output selected" (Oudiz and Sachs, 1984, p. 32).[9]

There are a few people in high places who recognize the intellectual validity of this analysis. But one of them (Feldstein, 1983) goes on the suggest:

> Economists armed with econometric models . . . can, under certain circumstances, identify coordinated policies that . . . are better than the outcome of uncoordinated policy choices. But, in practice, the overwhelming uncertainty about the quantitative behavior of individual economies and their interaction, the great difficulty of articulating policy rules in a changing environment, and the inevitable intervention of political factors . . . all make any such international fine-tuning unworkable.[10]

It is true that these models should be treated with considerable caution, especially because they are still not good at tracking exchange rates. But have we really reached the point where we need better models before we can agree on the obvious? For surely it must be obvious to all reasonable economists that there is something profoundly wrong with the national and international mix of monetary and fiscal policies currently being followed by the major industrial countries.

---

[9] It is encouraging to see the renewed academic interest in what is, or at least should be, a central focus of international macroeconomics. But see also my comments on Oudiz and Sachs (1984) in the same issue of *Brookings Papers on Economic Activity* (pp. 68-71).

[10] Earlier in the same article, Feldstein writes: "The United States has not allowed the fear of an increased current account deficit to limit our present or future rate of expansion." One cannot help wondering what is the "overwhelming uncertainty" about the inevitable consequences of this implicit assumption that there is *no* external constraint on American demand-management policies.

To those rightly concerned about reigniting inflation, it is obviously a mistake to have engineered a recovery in which over two-thirds of the increase in domestic demand has been generated in the United States, a country that accounts for less than one-third of the world GNP. This unnecessarily and prematurely puts at risk the anti-inflationary gains made in the United States.

To those rightly concerned about the erosion of capitalist virtues, it is obviously a mistake that these policies have unnecessarily prolonged very high and rising levels of unemployment in Europe. This has left more time for the Luddite forces there to do their deadly work—trying to "solve" the unemployment problem by using more people to produce the same output or telling people who would like to work more that, in the interest of others, they must work less.

To those rightly concerned about the development of the third world, and the need for more investment in the North, it is obviously a mistake to persist with a mix of monetary and fiscal policies that has produced abnormally high real interest rates during a necessary disinflation cure. (And, at the world level, the recovery is made even more lopsided and hence unsustainable by virtue of the fact that, for tax and other reasons, the American economy can live more easily than others with these high interest rates.)

To those rightly concerned about the real world of production and trade, and about the incessant struggle to resist the pressures for protectionism, subsidization, and "industrial policies," there is obviously something wrong with policies that have produced a 40 per cent real appreciation of the dollar in less than three years and that are so clearly sowing the seeds for an equally brutal decline at some point in the future.

If these propositions should be obvious to reasonable economists, why are they not obvious to those responsible for framing economic policy? The raison d'être of our profession is not just to satisfy our intellectual curiosity but to provide the analytical and empirical basis for better policies. If the policies are obviously wrong, it is not enough to blame politicians. We must also ask if there is not something wrong with our profession. We should teach students more history and read more ourselves. We should make more use of cross-country comparative analysis. We should remember that mathematics is a tool, not an end in itself, and that if ideas are to influence policymakers they must be translated from equations into the English language. We should resist the temptation to look constantly for new ideas that, almost by definition, are only third- or fourth-order qualifications to the things that really matter. Above all, we should concentrate more on synthesizing—in ways that can be understood by policymakers—those parts of our hard-won knowledge that have stood the test of time.

If we cannot do this, I fear that forty years from now another wise man will be writing something very similar to what Frank Graham (1942, p. 256) wrote over forty years ago: "The shadow . . . of natural law has . . . caused economic analysis to serve as the unwitting tool of a rationalization of things as they are. The science has become not only dismal, but slavishly discreet."

References

Aglietta, Michel, *Regulation et crises capitalistes: le cas des Etats-Unis*, Paris, Calmann Levy, 1977.
Artus, Jacques R., "An Empirical Evaluation of the Disequilibrium Real Wage Hypothesis," International Monetary Fund, processed, 1984.
Attali, Jacques, *Les trois mondes*, Paris, Arthème Fayard, 1981.

Blanchard, Olivier, and Rudiger Dornbusch, *U.S. Deficits, the Dollar and Europe*, Economic Papers No. 24, Brussels, Commission of the European Communities, 1983.
Branson, William H., and R. D. Hill, Jr., "Capital Movements in the OECD Area," *OECD Economic Outlook Occasional Studies*, Paris, December 1971.

Chouraqui, Jean-Claude, and Robert R. W. Price, "Medium-Term Financial Strategy: The Coordination of Fiscal and Monetary Policies," *OECD Economic Studies*, 2 (Spring 1984), pp. 7-49.
Cooper, Richard N., "Economic Interdependence and Coordination of Economic Policies," in Ronald W. Jones and Peter B. Kenen, eds., *Handbook of International Economics*, Amsterdam, North-Holland, forthcoming.

Dow, J. C. R., *The Management of the British Economy, 1945-60*, Cambridge, England, Cambridge University Press, 1964.

Feldstein, Martin, "Government Deficits and Aggregate Demand," *Journal of Monetary Economics*, 9 (January 1982), pp. 1-20.
———, "Martin Feldstein's Reply," *The Economist* (June 1983), p. 88.
Friedman, Milton, "The Case for Flexible Exchange Rates," in *Essays in Positive Economics*, Chicago, University of Chicago Press, 1953.

Giersch, Herbert, "Aspects of Growth, Structural Change, and Employment—A Schumpeterian Perspective," *Weltwirtschaftliches Archiv*, 115 (4, 1979).
Graham, Frank D., *Social Goals and Economic Institutions*, Princeton, N.J., Princeton University Press, 1942.
———, *Fundamentals of International Monetary Policy*, Essays in International Finance No. 2, Princeton, N.J., Princeton University, International Finance Section, 1943.

23

Graham, Frank D., "Full Employment Without Public Debt, Without Taxation, Without Public Works, and Without Inflation," in Abba P. Lerner and Frank D. Graham, eds., *Planning and Paying for Full Employment*, Princeton, N.J., Princeton University Press, 1946.

———, *The Cause and Cure of "Dollar Shortage,"* Essays in International Finance No. 10, Princeton, N.J., Princeton Univesity, International Finance Section, 1949.

Group of Ten, Communiqué issued after the May 12 Ministerial Meeting of the Group of Ten, *IMF Survey* (May 24, 1982), p. 149.

Hamada, Koichi, "Alternative Exchange Rate Systems and the Interdependence of Monetary Policies," in R. Aliber, ed., *National Monetary Policies and the International Financial System*, Chicago, University of Chicago Press, 1974.

———, "A Strategic Analysis of Monetary Interdependence," *Journal of Political Economy*, 84 (August 1976), pp. 677-700.

Johansen, Leif, "A Note on the Possibility of an International Equilibrium with Low Levels of Activity," *Journal of International Economics*, 13 (November 1982), pp. 257-267.

Johnson, Harry G., "The Case for Flexible Exchange Rates, 1969," in Harry G. Johnson and John E. Nask, eds., *UK and Floating Exchange Rates*, London, The Institute of Economic Affairs, 1969.

Larosière, J. de, "Restoring Fiscal Discipline," Speech given to the American Enterprise Institute, Washington, International Monetary Fund, Mar. 16, 1982.

Larsen, Flemming, John Llewellyn, and Stephen Potter, "International Economic Linkages," *OECD Economic Studies*, No. 1, 1983.

Lipietz, Alain, "Derrière la crise: la tendance à la baisse du taux de profit," *Revue Economique*, 2 (March 1982), pp. 197-231.

Malinvaud, E., *The Theory of Unemployment Reconsidered*, Oxford, Blackwell, 1977.

———, "Wages and Unemployment," *Economic Journal* (March 1982).

McKinnon, Ronald I., *An International Standard for Monetary Stabilization*, Policy Analyses in International Economics No. 8, Washington, Institute for International Economics, 1984.

Mundell, Robert A., "The Appropriate Use of Monetary and Fiscal Policy under Fixed Exchange Rates," *IMF Staff Papers*, Washington, D.C., March 1962.

Nurkse, Ragnar, *Conditions of International Monetary Equilibrium*, Essays in International Finance No. 4, Princeton, N.J., Princeton University, International Finance Section, 1945.

OECD, *The Balance of Payments Adjustment Process*, Report by Working Party No. 3 of the Economic Policy Committee, Paris, August 1966.

———, *Fiscal Policy for a Balanced Economy*, Report to the Council by Walter Heller, Cornelius Goedhart, Guillaume Guindey, Heinz Haller, Jean van Houtte, Assar Lindbeck, Richard Sayers, Sergio Steve, and J. C. R. Dow, 1968.

———, *Towards Full Employment and Price Stability*, Report to the Secretary-General by Paul McCracken, Guido Carli, Herbert Giersch, Attila Karaosmanoglu, Ryutaro Komiya, Assar Lindbeck, Robert Marjolin, and Robin Matthews, 1977.

——, *OECD Economic Outlook*, 34 (December 1983).

OEEC, *The Problem of Rising Prices*, Report to the Council by William Fellner, Milton Gilbert, Bent Hansen, Richard Kahn, Friedrich Lutz, and Pieter de Wolff, 1961.

Olson, Mancur, *The Rise and Decline of Nations*, New Haven, Conn., Yale University Press, 1982.

Oudiz, Gilles, and Jeffrey Sachs, "Macro-Economic Policy Co-ordination among the Industrial Economies," *Brookings Papers on Economic Activity* No. 1, 1984.

Radcliffe, *Report of the Committee on the Working of the Monetary System*, Cmnd. 827, HMSO, August 1959.

Sachs, Jeffrey D., "Wages, Profits and Macroeconomic Adjustment," *Brookings Papers in Economic Activity* No. 2, 1979.

——, "Real Wages and Unemployment in the OECD Countries," Brookings Papers on Economic Activity No. 1, 1983.

Solomon, Robert, *The International Monetary System 1945-1976*, New York, Harper & Row, 1977.

Vaubel, Roland, "Coordination or Competition among National Macroeconomic Policies?" in F. Machlup, G. Fels, and H. Muller-Groeling, eds., *Reflections on a Troubled World Economy*, London, 1983.

Williamson, John, *The Exchange Rate System*, Policy Analyses in Internationl Economics No. 5, Washington, Institute for International Economics, 1983.

Wolf, Martin, "A Rejoinder on the Question of How to Achieve Sustained Growth," *World Economy*, 4 (December 1983), pp. 440-445.

Yoshitomi, Masaru, "The Insulation and Transmission Mechanisms of Floating Exchange Rates Analyzed by the EPA World Model," Tokyo, Economic Planning Agency, March 1984, processed.

PUBLICATIONS OF THE
INTERNATIONAL FINANCE SECTION

Notice to Contributors

The International Finance Section publishes at irregular intervals papers in four series: ESSAYS IN INTERNATIONAL FINANCE, PRINCETON STUDIES IN INTERNATIONAL FINANCE, SPECIAL PAPERS IN INTERNATIONAL ECONOMICS, and REPRINTS IN INTERNATIONAL FINANCE. ESSAYS and STUDIES are confined to subjects in international finance. SPECIAL PAPERS are surveys of the literature suitable for courses in colleges and universities.

An ESSAY should be a lucid exposition of a theme, accessible not only to the professional economist but to other interested readers. It should therefore avoid technical terms, should eschew mathematics and statistical tables (except when essential for an understanding of the text), and should rarely have footnotes.

A STUDY or SPECIAL PAPER may be more technical. It may include statistics and algebra and may have many footnotes. STUDIES and SPECIAL PAPERS may also be longer than ESSAYS; indeed, these two series are meant to accommodate manuscripts too long for journal articles and too short for books.

To facilitate prompt evaluation, please submit three copies of your manuscript. Retain one for your files. The manuscript should be typed on one side of 8½ by 11 strong white paper. All material should be double-spaced—text, excerpts, footnotes, tables, references, and figure legends. For more complete guidance, prospective contributors should send for the Section's style guide before preparing their manuscripts.

How to Obtain Publications

A mailing list is maintained for free distribution of all new publications to college, university, and public libraries and nongovernmental, nonprofit research institutions.

Individuals and organizations not qualifying for free distribution can obtain ESSAYS and REPRINTS as issued and announcements of new STUDIES and SPECIAL PAPERS by paying a fee of $10 (within U.S.) or $12 (outside U.S.) to cover the period January 1 through December 31, 1984. Alternatively, for $30 they can receive all publications automatically—SPECIAL PAPERS and STUDIES as well as ESSAYS and REPRINTS.

ESSAYS and REPRINTS can also be ordered from the Section at $2.50 per copy, and STUDIES and SPECIAL PAPERS at $4.50. Payment MUST be included with the order and MUST be made in U.S. dollars. PLEASE INCLUDE $.80 FOR POSTAGE AND HANDLING. (These charges are waived on orders from persons or organizations in countries whose foreign-exchange regulations prohibit such remittances.) For airmail delivery outside U.S., Canada, and Mexico, there is an additional charge of $1.

All manuscripts, correspondence, and orders should be addressed to:

International Finance Section
Department of Economics, Dickinson Hall
Princeton University
Princeton, New Jersey 08544

Subscribers should notify the Section promptly of a change of address, giving the old address as well as the new one

27

List of Recent Publications

Some earlier issues are still in print. Write the Section for information.

ESSAYS IN INTERNATIONAL FINANCE

116. Weir M. Brown, *World Afloat: National Policies Ruling the Waves.* (May 1976)
*117. Herbert G. Grubel, *Domestic Origins of the Monetary Approach to the Balance of Payments.* (June 1976)
118. Alexandre Kafka, *The International Monetary Fund: Reform without Reconstruction?* (Oct. 1976)
119. Stanley W. Black, *Exchange Policies for Less Developed Countries in a World of Floating Rates.* (Nov. 1976)
120. George N. Halm, *Jamaica and the Par-Value System.* (March 1977)
121. Marina v. N. Whitman, *Sustaining the International Economic System: Issues for U.S. Policy.* (June 1977)
122. Otmar Emminger, *The D-Mark in the Conflict between Internal and External Equilibrium, 1948-75.* (June 1977)
*123. Robert M. Stern, Charles F. Schwartz, Robert Triffin, Edward M. Bernstein, and Walther Lederer, *The Presentation of the Balance of Payments: A Symposium.* (Aug. 1977)
*124. Harry G. Johnson, *Money, Balance-of-Payments Theory, and the International Monetary Problem.* (Nov. 1977)
*125. Ronald I. McKinnon, *The Eurocurrency Market.* (Dec. 1977)
126. Paula A. Tosini, *Leaning Against the Wind: A Standard for Managed Floating.* (Dec. 1977)
*127. Jacques R. Artus and Andrew D. Crockett, *Floating Exchange Rates and the Need for Surveillance.* (May 1978)
128. K. Alec Chrystal, *International Money and the Future of the SDR.* (June 1978)
129. Charles P. Kindleberger, *Government and International Trade.* (July 1978)
130. Franco Modigliani and Tommaso Padoa-Schioppa, *The Management of an Open Economy with "100% Plus" Wage Indexation.* (Dec. 1978)
131. H. Robert Heller and Malcolm Knight, *Reserve-Currency Preferences of Central Banks.* (Dec. 1978)
132. Robert Triffin, *Gold and the Dollar Crisis: Yesterday and Tomorrow.* (Dec. 1978)
133. Herbert G. Grubel, *A Proposal for the Establishment of an International Deposit Insurance Corporation.* (July 1979)
134. Bertil Ohlin, *Some Insufficiencies in the Theories of International Economic Relations.* (Sept. 1979)
135. Frank A. Southard, Jr., *The Evolution of the International Monetary Fund.* (Dec. 1979)

*Out of print. Available on demand in xerographic paperback or library-bound copies from University Microfilms International, Box 1467, Ann Arbor, Michigan 48106, United States, and 30-32 Mortimer St., London, WIN 7RA, England. Paperback reprints are usually $20. Microfilm of all Essays by year is also available from University Microfilms. Photocopied sheets of out-of-print titles are available on demand from the Section at $6 per Essay and $8 per Study or Special Paper.

136. Niels Thygesen, *Exchange-Rate Experiences and Policies of Small Countries: Some European Examples in the 1970s.* (Dec. 1979)
137. Robert M. Dunn, Jr., *Exchange Rates, Payments Adjustments, and OPEC: Why Oil Deficits Persist.* (Dec. 1979)
138. Tom de Vries, *On the Meaning and Future of the European Monetary System.* (Sept. 1980)
139. Deepak Lal, *A Liberal International Economic Order: The International Monetary System and Economic Development.* (Oct. 1980)
140. Pieter Korteweg, *Exchange-Rate Policy, Monetary Policy, and Real Exchange-Rate Variability.* (Dec. 1980)
141. Bela Balassa, *The Process of Industrial Development and Alternative Development Strategies.* (Dec. 1980)
142. Benjamin J. Cohen, *The European Monetary System: An Outsider's View.* (June 1981)
143. Marina v. N. Whitman, *International Trade and Investment: Two Perspectives.* (July 1981)
144. Sidney Dell, *On Being Grandmotherly: The Evolution of IMF Conditionality.* (Oct. 1981)
145. Ronald I. McKinnon and Donald J. Mathieson, *How to Manage a Repressed Economy.* (Dec. 1981)
*146. Bahram Nowzad, *The IMF and Its Critics.* (Dec. 1981)
147. Edmar Lisboa Bacha and Carlos F. Díaz Alejandro, *International Financial Intermediation: A Long and Tropical View.* (May 1982)
148. Alan A. Rabin and Leland B. Yeager, *Monetary Approaches to the Balance of Payments and Exchange Rates.* (Nov. 1982)
149. C. Fred Bergsten, Rudiger Dornbusch, Jacob A. Frenkel, Steven W. Kohlhagen, Luigi Spaventa, and Thomas D. Willett, *From Rambouillet to Versailles: A Symposium.* (Dec. 1982)
150. Robert E. Baldwin, *The Inefficacy of Trade Policy.* (Dec. 1982)
151. Jack Guttentag and Richard Herring, *The Lender-of-Last Resort Function in an International Context.* (May 1983)
152. G. K. Helleiner, *The IMF and Africa in the 1980s.* (July 1983)
153. Rachel McCulloch, *Unexpected Real Consequences of Floating Exchange Rates.* (Aug. 1983))
154. Robert M. Dunn, Jr. *The Many Disappointments of Floating Exchange Rates.* (Dec. 1983)
155. Stephen Marris, *Managing the World Economy: Will We Ever Learn?* (Oct. 1984)

PRINCETON STUDIES IN INTERNATIONAL FINANCE

44. Clas Wihlborg, *Currency Risks in International Financial Markets.* (Dec. 1978)
45. Ian M. Drummond, *London, Washington, and the Management of the Franc, 1936-39.* (Nov. 1979)
46. Susan Howson, *Sterling's Managed Float: The Operations of the Exchange Equalisation Account, 1932-39.* (Nov. 1980)
47. Jonathan Eaton and Mark Gersovitz, *Poor-Country Borrowing in Private Financial Markets and the Repudiation Issue.* (June 1981)

29

48. Barry J. Eichengreen, *Sterling and the Tariff, 1929-32*. (Sept. 1981)
49. Peter Bernholz, *Flexible Exchange Rates in Historical Perspective*. (July 1982)
50. Victor Argy, *Exchange-Rate Management in Theory and Practice*. (Oct. 1982)
51. Paul Wonnacott, *U.S. Intervention in the Exchange Market for DM, 1977-80*. (Dec. 1982)
52. Irving B. Kravis and Robert E. Lipsey, *Toward an Explanation of National Price Levels*. (Nov. 1983)
53. Avraham Ben-Bassat, *Reserve-Currency Diversification and the Substitution Account*. (March 1984)
54. Jeffrey Sachs, *Theoretical Issues in International Borrowing*. (July 1984)

SPECIAL PAPERS IN INTERNATIONAL ECONOMICS

8. Jagdish Bhagwati, *The Theory and Practice of Commercial Policy: Departures from Unified Exchange Rates*. (Jan. 1968)
*9. Marina von Neumann Whitman, *Policies for Internal and External Balance*. (Dec. 1970)
10. Richard E. Caves, *International Trade, International Investment, and Imperfect Markets*. (Nov. 1974)
*11. Edward Tower and Thomas D. Willett, *The Theory of Optimum Currency Areas and Exchange-Rate Flexibility*. (May 1976)
*12. Ronald W. Jones, *"Two-ness" in Trade Theory: Costs and Benefits*. (April 1977)
13. Louka T. Katseli-Papaefstratiou, *The Reemergence of the Purchasing Power Parity Doctrine in the 1970s*. (Dec. 1979)
*14. Morris Goldstein, *Have Flexible Exchange Rates Handicapped Macroeconomic Policy?* (June 1980)

REPRINTS IN INTERNATIONAL FINANCE

18. Peter B. Kenen, *Floats, Glides and Indicators: A Comparison of Methods for Changing Exchange Rates*. [Reprinted from *Journal of International Economics*, 5 (May 1975).] (June 1975)
19. Polly R. Allen and Peter B. Kenen, *The Balance of Payments, Exchange Rates, and Economic Policy: A Survey and Synthesis of Recent Developments*. [Reprinted from Center of Planning and Economic Research, Occasional Paper 33, Athens, Greece, 1978.] (April 1979)
20. William H. Branson, *Asset Markets and Relative Prices in Exchange Rate Determination*. [Reprinted from *Sozialwissenschaftliche Annalen*, Vol. 1, 1977.] (June 1980)
21. Peter B. Kenen, *The Analytics of a Substitution Account*. [Reprinted from *Banca Nazionale del Lavoro Quarterly Review*, No. 139 (Dec. 1981).] (Dec. 1981)
22. Jorge Braga de Macedo, *Exchange Rate Behavior with Currency Inconvertibility*. [Reprinted from *Journal of International Economics*, 12 (Feb. 1982).] (Sept. 1982)
23. Peter B. Kenen, *Use of the SDR to Supplement or Substitute for Other Means of Finance*. [Reprinted from George M. von Furstenberg, ed., *International Money and Credit: The Policy Roles*, Washington, IMF, 1983, Chap. 7.] (Dec. 1983)

ISBN 0-88165-062-5